# Whitwell

## History of a village

By

Joanne Thornton

Edited by Roger Ormisher

ISBN: 978-1-4092-5852-0

# Acknowledgements

I would like to thank the Isle of Wight records office for locating sources and the Ventnor Heritage centre for their help in locating sources and for postcards and pictures. I would also like to give a special thank you to Audrey New for the information and photographs she has provided for me on the village. In addition I would like to thank my family for their continued support.

# Contents

# Whitwell

The small village of Whitwell is situated in the south of the Isle of Wight; this village at one time had a coast line and was a part of the Undercliff. Whitwell remained a closed community throughout the Post Medieval period. The parish of Whitwell extended down to the coast in the pre-industrial period, as did all the parishes on the island. This was so that they all had some access to the coastal waters. Sir Richard Worsley wrote a book on the history of the Isle of Wight in 1781, this book contains the map on page 8; which shows the parish of Whitwell, in the $18^{th}$ century when it included Old Park, now a part of St Lawrence, and the farm of Wrongs, which is now in the sea.

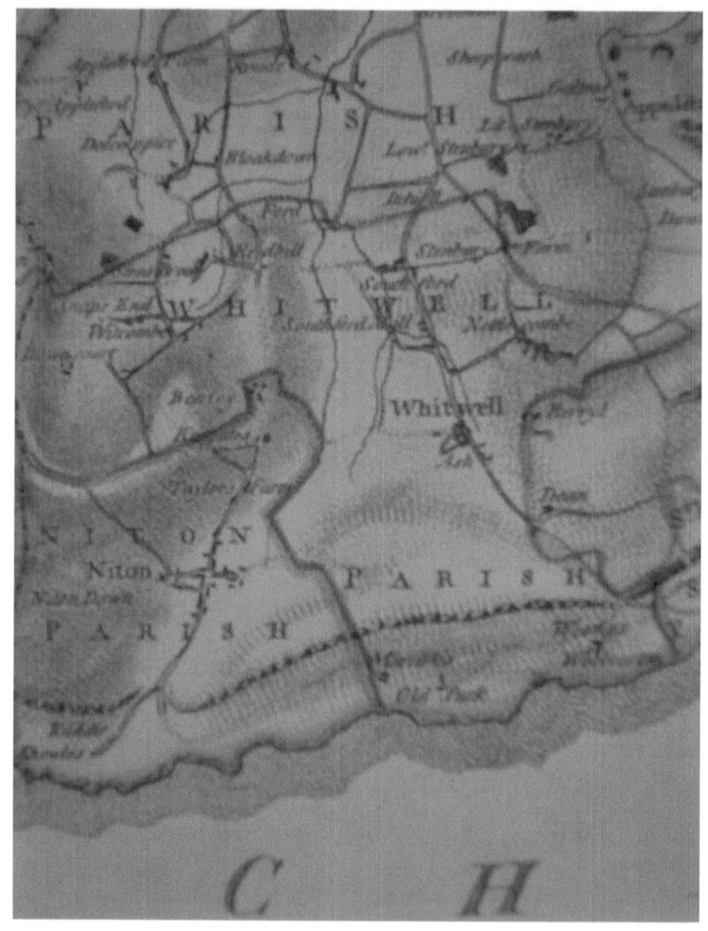


Migration was virtually non existent, and many did not leave the village their whole lives. Whitwell is mentioned in the Domesday book; it states that William of Stur holds Whitecombe (Whitcombe in Whitwell). It is recorded as having land for 1 plough, 2 ½ acres of meadow and was worth 15 shillings. Whitwell or Whytewell as it is called in 1297, was originally part of the Gatcombe estate. [1] The well in the village after which its name derives, is believed to have provided the pilgrim ships with 'white' water for their journeys to Poitiers and Compostelo. The water is thought to have healing properties. [2] The Pilgrim's way runs from the Undercliff between St Lawrence and Niton, up over the cliff on the Cripple Path, up behind the church and to the 'White' well.

A woman from Niton in c.1859, recalls her grandmother telling her that there used to be pilgrimages to the shrine of Our Lady of Whitwell and a famous crucifix; the pilgrims walked up the Cripple Path on their way to the shrine.[3]

As an agricultural community, Whitwell mainly consisted of farms. To the south of the village are 3 common fields; the upper and lower fields are divided each into 39 one acre or half acre strips. The third is the fallow or common field. The three field system was common in Medieval England. Two fields would be used for crops and the other would be left as fallow land, they would then be swapped around, so as the soil could have a break from growing crops and get back its nutrients as the fallow field for a year. To the Whitcombe side of Whitwell lay an upper and lower sheep common.[4]

The Nettlecombe area, which lies adjacent to Whitwell village, is the site of a Deserted Medieval Village. The name Nettlecombe indicates an early date, as combe or cwm is of Celtic origin.[5] Mounds and ditches exist in the fields, showing where people once lived and worked. The settlement of Nettlecombe is listed in the Domesday Book:

'*Nettlecombe, Hotelstone(e): King's land; Alric, his nephew and Humphrey from the king.*' [6]

A survey of the Worsley family estate in 1773 gives us an insight into the village and it's layout in the mid 18th century.[7] The map shown on page 12 is based on the 1773 survey, showing the relative positions of houses in Whitwell at that time. The buildings shown on the map are listed in an accompanying survey book, which is located at the Isle of Wight record office. Some of the buildings have been marked on the map.

Many of the properties that are marked still exist as dwellings today. The buildings retain some of their original features from the late 18th century, but as with many buildings, have undergone alteration of some kind since this time. It was the land in the 18th century that was named not the dwelling house, so houses built and rebuilt on the same spot often retained the name of the previous dwelling in that area. Many of the dwellings were named after those renting the land. This land usually stayed in families, and the name therefore ran through many generations.

There are many links between the Yeoman families of Whitwell to those of Niton; the names of Jacob, Ston and Hardley exist in both villages.[8] Looking back through the Worsley steward's accounts and old leases, one can see that the vast majority of the buildings named on the map were once occupied by people of that name. The map also shows Slay Lane coming down to the High Street. This was changed in recent years when the new houses were built on that road; the new road of Bannock Road was built down from the original Slay Lane to meet the High Street.

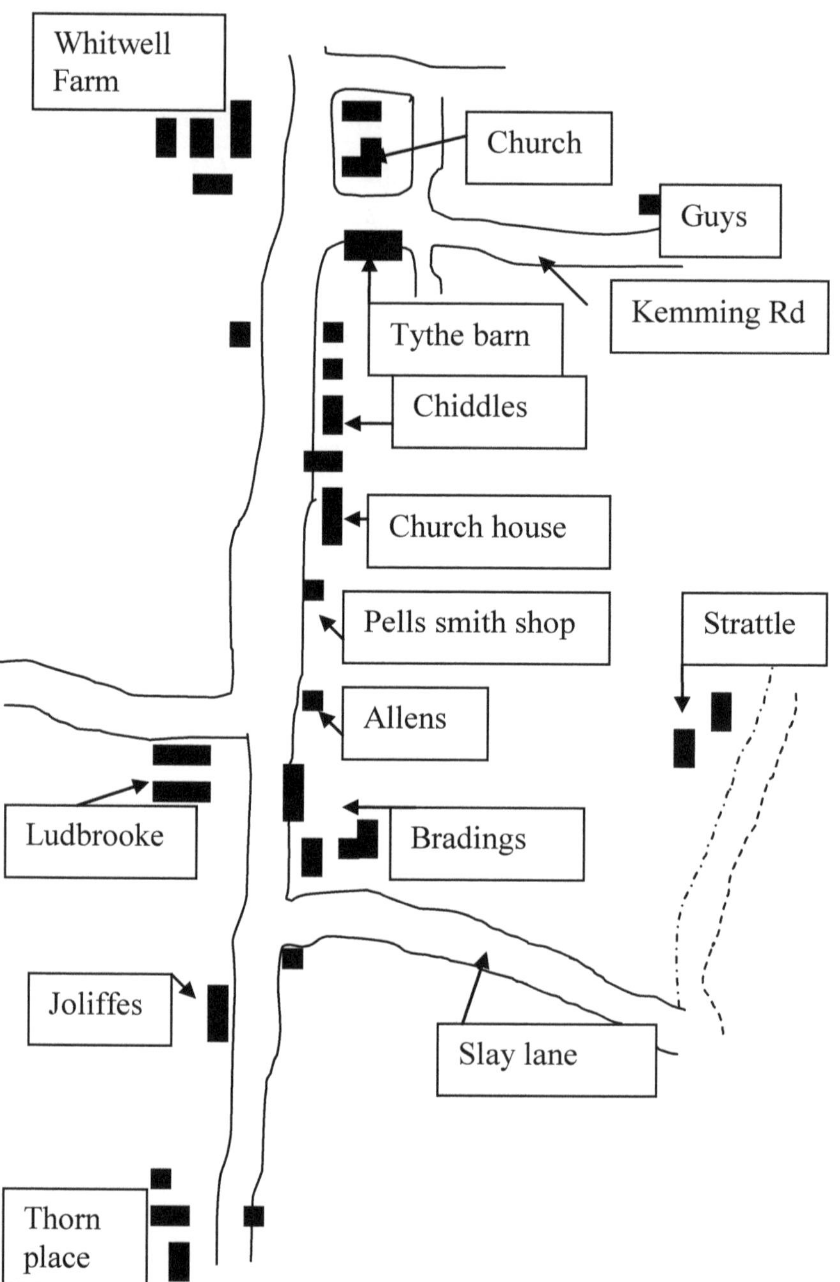
Whitwell Farm
Church
Guys
Kemming Rd
Tythe barn
Chiddles
Church house
Pells smith shop
Strattle
Allens
Ludbrooke
Bradings
Joliffes
Slay lane
Thorn place

The 1838 Tythe map shows an increase in the buildings of Whitwell, alongside adaptations and extensions to a number of houses. This can be viewed along with the Tythe schedule in the Isle of Wight records office. A history of the development of Whitwell can clearly be seen in the record of maps available. From the early modern period to the Victorian period, Whitwell experienced growth not just in the number of houses being built, but from an increase in the variety of trades and services available. The railway in 1897 brought a rapid increase in trade to the once tiny self-sufficient community.

# Earning a living.

The village was under the jurisdiction of the Lord of Appledurcombe in the 17th and 18th centuries, the seat of Appledurcombe was held by the Worsleys at this time. The Lord of the Manor would have provided work and taken on the services of the local community which would have included Whitwell. The Lord would purchase his supplies and food from local farmers as well as growing his own. Evidence for this can be seen in the Steward's account books.

Buying locally, the Lord, Sir Robert Worsley at this time, ordered 20 butts of oats from John Holbrook in 1717 paying £1 3s for them; He paid Farmer Hailes 18s for mead, and in 1718 paid Knowles £1 9s for shrimps and flatfish and in 1719 13s 6d for crabs and lobsters.

In 1719 the Worsleys also paid for 20 quarters of Barley to be malted in the spring, this cost them £14. £5 12s was also paid for bottles and corks.[9] The fish from Knowles probably came from Knowles Farm on the coast at Niton, showing that the Worsley's would source food from around the Whitwell area.

Whitwell village has the remains of a Tythe barn, this stands opposite the church, on Kemming Road. This barn was where the villagers would have stored their produce. The Tythe or 10% would have been passed on to the landlord as rent or to those who had brought the Tythe rights for particular pieces of land. Tythe's were an ancient custom, which were referred to in the bible; this tells how a tenth of field produce each year should be stored in the town, this was the Tythe. [10] The idea of Tythes came to England with St Augustine and by the end of the 12th Century they were compulsory. Tythe barns were constructed to hold the village produce[11] and typically it would have been the Lord of the Manor who collected the 10% 'Tythe tax.' This image shows the Tythe barn, before it was partially demolished.

The remains of the Whitwell Tythe barn as it stands on the corner of Kemming Road today.

Although agriculture was the main occupation for those living in Whitwell during the early modern period; carting and the building of houses was a way for some to earn extra income. The Worsley's would have used the local labour force for their building work, and their account books detail bills paid out for building work and associated tasks.

From Oct 1720-May 1721, Ed Hardy was carting and received £12 10s for his trouble; carting was where a 2 wheeled cart, pulled by a horse was used to transport goods. Coleman was paid £9 for carting 40 tons of stone from the Undercliffe to Appledurcombe; Will Spanner was paid £3 13s for carting stone and timber. The Spanner's occupied a cottage in Niton of 3 bays, and had a barn of 4 bays. The dwelling was known as Upper Burdge in 1581; when the value of the lease was £6. [12] Whereas, Goody Moozes was paid for weeding and picking stones between Sept 1720 and May 1721; this shows the kind of labour a woman may be able to pick up in the winter months when agricultural work would be at a minimum. Similarly Goody Davis was paid £1 11s 6.5d for haying and wooding at Appledurcombe House. She was also weeded the garden at Appledurcombe.

Money was different back in the 18th century and was expressed in pounds, shillings and pence. One shilling was equal to 12 pennies and 20 shillings was equal to a pound. [13] The average daily wage for a labourer at this time was about 15-20 pence. Craftsmen were looking at slightly more with 22-36 pence on average per day. [14] If this was converted into current coinage, without taking into account inflation, then it would be about equivalent to £20-25 a year for a labourer and £30-35 for a skilled building craftsman. [15] The cost of living was roughly in line with the wages, but a major expense was the rent of property, and around £40 was the average needed to support a family.[16] Extra work especially around harvest could be done to boost up earnings or other members of the family could work to contribute towards the cost of living.

Money paid out by the Lord of the Manor, Sir Worsley, shows a variety of trades and the charges that were made for services required at the manor. This can give an idea of the kind of money that these tradesmen expected for their services. The thatching of Redhill House for example cost £1 2s in 1717, whereas Mr Orchard was paid 6s 6d for tailor's work, and Mr Whitwood was paid 7s for farrier's work. The bill from a saddlers came to £1 7s 9d, while the bill for some basketwork came to £2 2s 6d.[17]

Not only do these examples give us information on the types of work people were doing in the areas surrounding Whitwell in the 18th century, but they also inform us about the kind of prices people were willing to spend on materials. For example John Allys paid 19s for paving stones for his new malt house, Mr Hunt was paid for 3000 sap lathes and for slate £1 17s 6d, while Mr Teattle was paid 15s for lime, and Mr Paine, £2 4s for straw in 1721.

In addition, these accounts detail how much people were willing to pay for labour; in 1723, Mr Allen was paid £14

11s 7d for work that he undertook at the stable of Week Farm and for work he did at Will Spanner's. Mr Allen seems to have taken on quite a bit of building work, and is recorded as being paid for building barns, a stable, and a carthouse. In addition, he was paid for lath and plastering a dwelling house. All this work earnt him £31 6s 2d. He was also paid £11 3s 6d for building a brew house at Sheep Wash Farm in the same year.

# Cottages in Whitwell

The village contains many old cottages dating back to the 17th and 18th centuries. The land on which a cottage was built was the name which was given in the rent books. This name was for the particular area of land, and often, particularly in the Medieval and up to about the $18^{th}$ century, cottages would be rebuilt several times on the same piece of land. It was not until cottages began to be made from more durable materials, that they remained more permanent features. Therefore not all the cottages mentioned would have remained the same as they were when first built and many have been significantly altered.

In 1560, there is a record of several properties in Whitwell, alongside the Church House and a watermill.[18] In 1586, there is a record of the property Mill Place alias Midleford which was occupied by John Longe. In 1802 a shoemakers is shown as being leased by William Read, who also rented the land called Guys.[19] The cottage of Kemmen, alias Kinell is first mentioned in 1675 occupied by William Newberry.[20] A lease dated 1615, records a house newly built in Whitwell with a garden lying to the south of the Church House. This was built by Richard Jacobe with permission from the churchwardens of the time.[21] Churchwardens were well respected members of the local community; they kept accounts, and were often Yeomen farmers; these were farmers that owned their own land.[22]

A cottage near the Church House is mentioned in a lease dated 1680, this is occupied by John Searle and James Howe, both Church wardens. [23] John Searle is also known to have paid the lease on Bradings Farm in 1677; [24] Bradings Farm is often given alongside Ludbrookes and Allens as a group; according to the will of George King, this group of dwellings was collectively called Bridge. A lease from 1773 gives George King as occupying Bridge Farm.[25] A lease of 1708 however, gives the dwelling of Ludbridge alias Ludbrookes.[26] It could be that once all three dwellings were known as Ludbrookes, or Ludbridge, as evidence exists of a north, south and east Ludbrookes. North Ludbrooke is mentioned in the leases for the first time in 1637 when it is occupied by William Brading;[27] this could be an early reference to Brading farm. Allens which lies to the south of Brading Farm was also known as South Ludbrooke;[28] North Ludbrooke is mentioned in 1638, alongside a property called Brockwell, these are both occupied by John Brading [29] Whereas East Ludbrooke also mentioned in 1638 is occupied by Ann Newnam.[30] This property is to the east of Bradings and Allens. It is possible that there was once a bridge connecting all three properties; as Bradings farm, and Allens lie on the opposite side of the river to Ludbrookes. The dwellings of Bridge are also mentioned in a 1688 lease, alongside Strattle, Stockbridge, Kemmen, Spanners hold, Newberry, Gotten, Bromans, Morgans and Hayles. [31] The cottages of Bradings and Allens will be examined later .

**The Forge**

In 1699 we know there was a smith's shop occupied by Mary Pell,[32] this later became the forge. The term smith, originates from the word smite; this means to hit, and a blacksmith will hit or smite the metal to shape it. In 1712 the annual rent for Pells smith shop was 2s; it was occupied by a Mr Woodnutt at this time.[33] In 1778, James Russell was paying the rent on Pells still at 2s. [34] The forge is where the fire used by the blacksmith was controlled. The far left side of the south gable shows random rubble which could be part of the earlier Pell's smith shop. Other builds or coursed rubble have been added as the use has changed. The forge is now a residential building.

The forge, when occupied by Ted Atkey. Farmer Lowe, of Southford farm having his horse shod.

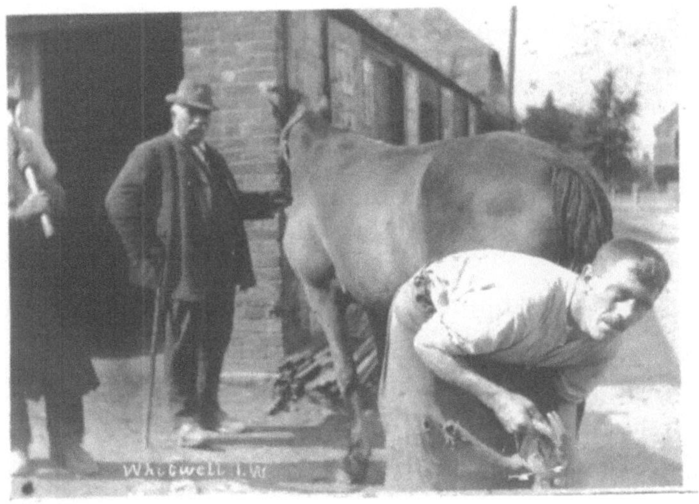


The forge as it stands in the village today

**Farms**

Whitwell, being an agricultural community had a large number of farms; these were leased from the Lord of the Manor. The vast majority of the villagers would have been involved in some way with farming. If they did not earn enough to lease their own land, then they would work for a farmer that did. In addition, there was a mill, and no doubt would have been a bakery where villagers could have their bread baked.

In 1676, Southford Farm was occupied by Richard Harvey who was paying rent of 15s a year;[35] in 1703 it is recorded as being occupied by a Thomas Hardly.[36] In 1773 Southford is occupied by John Sanders. Ford Farm is situated at the northern end of Whitwell, it was farmed by the Attrills. The pictures on page 25 show Ford Farm and the surrounding farmland.

The Ford was situated nearby, this is where the farm got its name.

The watermill at Ford Farm.

Ford mill is no longer in use. It was a corn mill, and once owned by St Helen's priory. It dates back to at least 1558. The pictures show the mill in the early 20$^{th}$ century. In 1729 there is a mill recorded at Southford; Southford Mill was occupied by the miller, Thomas Cook. In 1778, the rent was for a moiety of Southford mill; a moiety is a part of the mill, and the water acres was occupied by David Jones, who paid 11s 6d a year in rent.[37] There was also a mill at Bridgecourt, which is near to Godshill. Water acres are also known as water meadows; these were used to keep fields damp, water from a stream was channelled to flow through terraces down gently sloping fields. In 1773 Strattle farm was occupied by Philip Caws, Thornplace Farm by Robert Young, Aylesbury Farm by John Sanders, Willistones farm by William Harvey, Leigh's Farm by Robert Young and Old Park Farm by Mary Harvey[38]

In 1712 the rent on Thornplace is 18s and 4s for Burstoes.[39] In 1778, they are listed together with the rent of £1 4s being paid by a Mr White. [40] The cottages that currently stand where Thornplace and Burstoes are located on the 1773 survey map stand at the far north end of the High Street.

Further down the lane to the south stands another thatched cottage. This was the cottage that belonged to Joliffe according to the 1773 map; it is now know as the Brookside cottages. In 1778 Henry Roach was paying rent of 18s for the Joliffe's farm.

This is the Brookside Cottages, at the north end of the High Street.

The architecture of the cottages reveal that there were additional doors and windows at some point that have been blocked. The cottage has been much altered over the past few hundred years, now consisting of 3 dwellings. A dripstone still exists over one of the cottage doors. This was to stop the water running down from the thatch directly over the door, adding protection to the wood. In addition there is timber framing in evidence over the southern side of the building, this will be remains from a previous build.

In 1730, there is a lease for a Whitwell Farm, alias Falchbarne and Ashe. In 1778 Whitwell Farm was purchased for £4025; today it is a village home on the High Street.

**Chiddles/White Horse**

The dwelling house Chiddles is first mentioned in 1676 when rent was paid at 2s 3d a year.[41] In 1712 the cottage of Late Chiddles was occupied by Combs and rent paid of 7s 6d per year.[42] In 1773, it was leased by John Bundell; in 1778, it was still occupied by Mr Bundell and he paid a rent of 1s 6d a year. [43] It was then taken over by Richard Cooke, a Brewer in 1780. [44] The differences in the rates charged for rent, could be due to more, or less, land being leased with the dwelling house or extensions being added or demolished. The property is originally shown on the 1773 survey map by the Worsley's and in 1560 Alice Chidlee is recorded as living in Whitwell [45] A mention is also given to a lease on a dwelling occupied by a Henry Chedyll, in 1596 both of which could later have become Chiddles. [46] The White Horse ale house is first mentioned in a lease dated 1804.[47]

The right hand side of the pub was once the stable area, while the central area was the cottage formally known as Chiddles. The left hand extension is a much more modern extension. The central area is of random rubble, whereas the right hand side is more coursed rubble; the stone has been lime washed. The building was previously thatched but this was replaced with slate in 2007 after a fire broke out in 2006.

By Comparison, an inn at Steephill, in the early 1800s that accommodated much of the gentry that were visiting the Undercliffe, was a small cottage with a shed for the kitchen and tap room. There were also tents pitched in the garden to accommodate a greater number of people. This may have been similar in layout to the White Horse in its early years. [48]

## The Church House

In 1596, the Church House was occupied by John Langford and William Smyth, the clerk. [49] In 1676 the rent on church house was 2s 6d. [50] In 1712 the Whitwell quarter are recorded as paying the rent of 1s 8d for church house. [51] The Whitwell quarter is another term for the area known as Whitwell; it is a non-administrative but distinctive district.

The Church House was ' provided always that if the quarter shall need at any time to make a quarter-ale or church-ale for the maintenance of the chapel, that it shall be lawful for them to have the use of the house with all the rooms, both above and beneath during their ale.' [52]

By 1723, the Whitwell quarter ceased to pay the lease for the Church houses and they were rented by the then churchwarden William Gillingham. [53] By 1778 George King was paying the rent for Church House and a cottage at 5s a year. [54]

The building is lime washed and built using random rubble. There are drip stones over some of the windows in the north gable. The dripstone above the window on the northern gable is shown below.

Church houses were used by the church to sell ale to the community. The church wardens would sell ale, like the coffee mornings of today, to raise money for church funds.

**The 1721/22/23 cottages**

There are three cottages in Whitwell that bear date stones; 1721, 1722 and 1723. The cottage bearing 1722 was once known as Brading Farm and is now Strathwell Dale. It was a dairy at the turn of the century, and is recorded in the Kelly's Directory as Brading Farm in 1921-22, occupied by Mr Albert Allen, and in 1923 the building is recorded as Strathwell cottage still occupied by Mr Allen. [55] After the 1870s there were various depressions in the farming trade. The property of Brading does not appear in the Kelly's Directory before 1921 as a dairy, and therefore was probably a farmhouse. Many farmers turned their farms into a dairy when farming became less profitable, as the depression brought down prices of their goods.[56]

In the late 18th century, the property was leased by George King, when it had a malt house and brew house. George King was a large landowner in the village, holding property alongside Sir Richard Worsley. In addition to the many acres of land, he held Church House, and the two adjoining cottages, Ludbrookes and Allens.[57] George King also held an indenture of lease for the chapel at 10 shillings and 6d. This passed to his daughters when he died. Furthermore, Ralph Stone was recorded as having leased Bradings farm[58]; Ralph was the local hero of the early 19th century, due to the number of smuggling adventures he is said to have had. Mishaps did occur, even for Ralph, as he spent several periods in Winchester gaol for being a 'debtor to the crown'. When he died he left to his heirs considerable property including Bradings Farm that he had accrued from the illicit trade he had been running. [59]

The tenement of Bradings can be traced back to 1677 in the Worsley estate account books. Therefore, a dwelling house has existed on this site since that time, and whether or not any of the original building remains is not certain. Many early cottages were constantly rebuilt. [60] There are pieces of stone in the walls of this building which are shaped and have been reused in the building of Bradings Farm. The 1722 date could have been when alterations or rebuilding occurred on the house. A partition, to separate the kitchen to what was to become the dairy seems to date from this time. This building has three gables in the roof, which were probably added in the Victorian period, when the gothic revival style became popular.

This was perhaps when the roof was slated. Originally the building would have been thatched. This can be seen by the steep pitch of the roof, and the coping with kneelers on the end gables of the house.

The house is now divided into two properties, Strathwell Dale, and Brading Cottage. Strathwell Dale being the older part of the original building and Brading Cottage was built as an extension sometime between 1773, when it is not shown on the Worsley estate survey map; and 1838, where the extension is shown on the Tythe map. The extension of Brading Cottage has a pegged clay tile roof, in addition there are blocked off windows and a door facing into what would have been a courtyard with Strathwell Dale. The windows have a brick surround. The picture below shows Brading Cottage as an extension coming off the back of Strathwell Dale.

The house bearing 1723 was once the old Post Office, and there are mentions of a dwelling on that site in 1630 as previously stated when Richard Jacobe built his house to the south of the Church House, where this building is situated. Therefore, the same can be said of this house, that it was perhaps rebuilt or altered in 1723. The old Post Office can be seen on page 40 with the bow window still in place that once acted as the Grocers shop. Early Grocers shops were not as they are today; they sold goods by the gross, and often acted as drapers shops as well. [61] Drapers were concerned with the sale of cloth and dry goods. Drapers also commonly sold haberdashery; items such as ribbons or lace to adorn clothing.

The house bearing the 1721 date stone is now called Union Cottage. This building could also be older than the date stone; an extension has been added to the right side to give extra room.

The date stones are similar in style and two have the same initials engraved. The initials were sometimes the builder or sometimes could be the initials of the husband and wife. The date stones 1722 and 1723 are very similar in style, with 1721 still the same layout, but the style is not quite the same.

R E
1722

1723

**Allens**

The property Allens, stands to the south of Brading Farm. There is a property recorded on that spot in 1677, when John Allen is recorded as paying rent on a property called Allens in the Worsley account books. He is recorded as paying 4s 6d for the years lease. [62] In 1712 the rent is paid by Mr Symonds for late Allens still at 4s 6d per year. Below is a picture of the property today. This is now known as Bayleaf Cottage, and was previously Chapel Cottage named as such when the Methodist chapel was built opposite.

The house used to be two buildings that were separated by a narrow passageway. The main building being the stem of the L shape, and the end of the L being once a one up, one down cottage. Evidence of the join between the two can be seen in the stone work of the cottage. The one up one down cottage must have been built at a later time than the other part of the building however, as the 1773 survey map does not show this part of the building; Whereas the 1838 Tythe map does show a section coming off to form an L.

**Strathwell**

Strattle is recorded as being occupied by Mr Newnham in 1712 at a rent of 16s 4d. [63] In 1778, it is still occupied by the Newnhams and a woman named Ann is listed as the rent payer at 13s per year. This could perhaps be due to her now having less land or being a widow. The house would not be listed in a woman's name unless she was widowed and the land left to her by her husband's will. [64]

Strattle cottage as shown on the 1773 survey map is located on the site of the now Strathwell House. Strathwell house was built by the Rector of Whitwell. In 1881 the head of Strathwell House is recorded in the census as being Catherine Covey, who is the sister-in-law to the head of the household. There are two sons and a daughter that are Willnett's living there, and a nephew, in addition to: a governess, two domestic nurses, a parlour maid, a housemaid and a coachman. In the 1891 census the recorded inhabitants of Strathwell are Mr Willett, a magistrate and his family, there was also a caretaker, Mr Chiverton and his wife, and the coachman, William Russell and his family. Mrs Willett was recorded as head of the household at Strathwell in 1898, so presumably Mr Willett had died by this point. [65]

Below is Strathwell House as it stands today in Strathwell Park.

# Popular Religion and custom

The church at Whitwell is somewhat unique in that it used to be two separate chapels that were made into just one church. The chapel of St Rhadegund was built by the Gatcombe estate in the 12th century, and the altar was raised to St Rhadegund. St Rhadegund was a German Princess, she had become a nun and gave her life to the poor and needy; she was the patron saint of the Stur family. William Fitz Stur held Gatcombe in the time of King Edward the Confessor.[66] This chapel did not have an aisle, but one narrow chancel. The Chapel of St Rhadegund was served by the Rector of Gatcombe, who kept up repairs and took the Tythes.

The chapel of St Mary was built by the Lords of Stenbury, and may have been built for the Montebourg tenants of Wydcombe. The chapel of St Mary's was served by Godshill and kept in repair by the inhabitants of Whitwell. In 1515, it was agreed by decree that the Parishes of Gatcombe and Godshill were to provide a Rector to reside at Whitwell that would please them both.[67] The wall between the two chapels was removed in the 16th century; it was a recommendation from Cromwell's commissioners. [68] The tower was also built at this time. [69]

Whitwell was not a parish in the seventeenth century; the two chapels were 'chapels of ease.' [70] Chapels of ease were built for the use of villagers when the main parish church was not very accessible to them. The main church would have been Godshill for the villagers using the chapel serviced by the Godshill curate. With the other's main parish church being at Gatcombe. [71] Whitwell was given a vicarage in 1867 when the livings of Godshill and Whitwell were separated. [72]

The church shows two different building styles, coursed rubble and ashlar. The tower is of ashlar with some of the older areas of the chapel coursed rubble. Ashlar was usually reserved for better quality properties, as it was more expensive than rubble.

Whitwell also has a healing well, after which the village gets its name. It is said that pilgrims came from St Lawrence, where they arrived in boats, and then walked to Whitwell along the Pilgrims Way, and Cripple Path, so-called because of the people who walked it to be healed by the well. The well today has a grating over it, and is located opposite the church.

Well dressing is an ancient custom that is rarely seen today, and the wells of St Lawrence and Whitwell on the Isle of Wight join only a handful of others across the country, mainly in Derbyshire, that still celebrate this ancient rite.

The well is dressed every year by village residents, and was introduced by the Reverend Sandra Lloyd in 2002, to celebrate the Pilgrims Way and to give villagers a closer link to the community. [73] The Reverend Lloyd and her team travelled up to Derbyshire in order to learn the technique from the villagers.

The 2007 well dressing is shown above, commemorating 110 years since the Whitwell railway was built. Each year, a local or national event, or anniversary is chosen to be commemorated by the well dressing. In 2006 the well dressing was of the fire at the White Horse pub. This was a significant event in the village, as not only was one of the oldest buildings in the village in danger of being destroyed, but the pub lost it's thatched roof, having it replaced with slate to prevent further fire hazards from the straw.

This well dressing shows the fire fighters battling the flames to save the pub.

The Well dressing in 2004 was Saint Joan of Arc.

Well dressing originates from Pagan times, when wells were blessed to keep the water clean. These practices were adopted by the Christian faith, and wells were blessed once a year, and turned into Christian holy wells. The well at Whitwell is still blessed by the church annually. The pressing of petals into the design on a clay plaque is of recent origin, this came about in the early nineteenth century. Previously, garlands of flowers and boughs of trees were used to decorate the wells. [74] The wooden boards used in the Whitwell dressing are soaked in the old sheep dip stream, this helps to prevent the clay from drying out too quickly, thus preserving the dressing for longer. The design is marked out on the clay with coffee beans before the materials are added to build up the design. [75]

There is evidence for a dissenting community being in existence in Whitwell; Dissenters were followers of the Christian faith, but did not agree with the teachings of the Church of England. From 1786 a meeting house certificate was issued for meetings to be held in the house of Peter Crew at Nettlecombe. [76] In 1815, another certificate was issued, this time for meetings to be held in the barn of William Hollier. [77] In 1824 a certificate was issued for meetings to be held at the house of William Young and William Strongman of St Helens, minister; this time it was specified that the meetings were for a Methodist group.[78] Furthermore, in 1824 a certificate was issued for a Baptist group to hold meetings at the house of Robert Grace. [79] In 1834 another certificate was issued for meetings to be held in the house of James Harvey and Harry

Major, minister of Portsea; [80] this is the last listed certificate, the Bible Christians chapel was built in 1846

A United Methodist Chapel was built in 1884; this is now a private residence. There was also a room that was licensed for various groups of dissenters. [81] In the 18th century, lots of chapels and meeting houses were built by the dissenting community; many were built of red brick, as the one in Whitwell was. They provided fetes and outings for their congregations, and proved to be popular in villages, rapidly becoming social centres. [82] This image is of the United Methodist chapel, located in the north end of the High Street.

Other customs existed in Whitwell, and other villages on the Isle of Wight; the letters of John Green, once written for the Isle of Wight Mercury in 1890 tells of the custom when he was a boy, to rub wounds with the hand of a dead person in order to cure the wound.[83] It was believed that the wound would diminish as the corpse rotted in the grave. There has been found evidence of what is believed to be a protective charm in the roof of what was once Brading farm alias Strathwell Dale. A lock of hair was found between the tie beam and principal rafters during an archaeological survey. This is shown on page 57.

The hair is auburn in colour and was twisted into a lock when discovered. It is about 12 inches in length. It is not unusual to find protective charms in older buildings.

Many people believed in witchcraft or the evil eye in earlier times; these charms were used to help ease the mind of the villagers. It is thought that finds of hidden objects containing human remains such as hair, act as some kind of decoy for malefic forces to attack instead of the house occupiers.[84]

A preventative measure used in the Orkney Islands at Yuletide appears to be similar; to prevent livestock from becoming targets of the evil eye a cross was made from 2 pieces of straw, from this was hung plaited hair from the tail of each cow. The plaited hair was then hung over the byre door to protect the animals inside. This same practice was used in the Orkneys's to protect food and ale in the house. Crosses were put over the food and a sheaf of corn put in the roof to guard from malevolent spirits. [85]

Witch bottles and hidden objects such as shoes and even mummified cats have been found in old buildings across the British Isles. Hidden either in chimneys, roofs or under the floor, these objects show the force and power believed to exist in charms and protective amulets. There are two other recorded examples of concealed objects in buildings on the Isle of Wight. A mummified cat was found in a chimney in St Helens,[86] and a collection of 3 boots and a man's patten was found under the floorboards at Haseley Manor, Arreton. [87] A Patten is similar to a clog and was worn in Medieval times. Shoes were commonly hidden in buildings, particularly in roofs, under floorboards or up chimneys; it is thought that they were hidden in openings to ward off evil spirits. Shoes were usually well worn and sometimes other objects were concealed alongside them. They are rarely found in pairs, but families of single shoes are sometimes found.[88]

The Steward Account books also tell of another custom in the Whitwell area at Christmas. In the early 18th century it must have been custom for the Lord of the Manor to provide the poor with a bull at Christmas time. The accounts show that it cost 14s for the bull to be killed and dressed. [89] The recollections of John Green from the late 18th century describe how the farmer of Chale Farm would measure out wheat and give one gallon each to the poor women of the parish on 21st December each year, which was St Thomas' day.[90]

A charity called King's Gift belongs to the parish of Whitwell. This gift was left to the parish by Fanny King, the widow of

George King in her will of 1808. To the Rector and Churchwardens of the parish, she gave £50 on trust; this was to be invested in government, and the interest was to be used to buy bread. This bread was to be distributed at the church on the Sunday after Christmas day among the poor of the parish according to their need. [91]

# The Victorian age

In the late 19th century Brannon wrote of Whitwell:

*'Whitwell is a retired and very pretty village between Godshill and Niton, but rarely passed through by strangers making the regular tour of the island. The church is an ancient plain structure with a handsome square tower, conspicuously seen from some of the neighbouring highroads.'* [92]

Before the coming of the railway, transport into and out of Whitwell was limited. Roads were not good and walking would have been one of the main ways to travel, with horse riding for those that were rich enough to own one. There was a carrier service that operated out of Whitwell to the main county town of Newport. In 1859, William and Robert Jones are the carriers operating the service to Newport. [93] In 1865, Robert Jones was the carrier to the Plough Inn, Newport; his service ran Monday, Wednesday and Saturday. [94] In 1898 the carrier to Newport was run to the George Inn by William Oliver Norris on Wednesdays and Saturdays. [95] Carriers had horse drawn carts or covered wagons, sometimes with rough benches to carry those villagers wishing to go to the towns. The main job of many carriers was to take goods to market for village producers, and to bring back orders for villagers. [96] This picture gives an example of what a carrier's wagon would have looked like. This carrier is one from Ventnor to Carisbrooke.

The poorer passengers would have sat on the roof, with the richer passengers who could afford a more comfortable ride inside the carriage.

The railway line at Whitwell was opened in 1897, and was part of the Ventnor West line, running to Merstone.[97] It was the last railway line to be built on the island. The line only went as far as St Lawrence in 1897, but was extended to Ventnor West, then called Ventnor Town in 1900.

This picture shows the Ventnor West line being built in 1893.

The Whitwell railway station is situated in Nettlecombe Lane.

Whitwell was the crossing point of this line and had a 402 ft 6 inch crossing loop. There was an up platform and a down platform. The Station Master's House and the booking office were situated on the up platform. [98] At Dean there was a level crossing with a pedestrian bridge.

In October 1909, the passenger train arrived at Whitwell to go to Ventnor at 12.18, 13.31 and 17.45 with a service on Saturdays running at 21.33. On Sundays a mixed service ran at 9.40 and a passenger service at 20.45. Running from Whitwell to Merstone the passenger train departed Whitwell at 9.55, 11.03, 12.45, 16.53, 18.08, and 20.48, with a Saturday service running at 21.53. On Sundays, the mixed service departed Whitwell at 10.44, and the passenger service departed at 21.08. In the summer of 1939, the passenger train was much more regular with stops nearly every hour from 7 am till 9 pm, in both directions. The Sunday service was still reduced with only 3 services running each way.

An idea of the cost of travelling on the railway can be gleaned from the old tickets. A third class fare from Ventnor West to Whitwell cost 6d; Whitwell to St Lawrence cost 4 ½ d; From Godshill to Whitwell third class cost 5d. A monthly third class fare between Whitwell and Ventnor West was 7 1/2 d. [99] The Ventnor West line closed down in 1952.

The tunnel that once ran from Whitwell to St Lawrence remains, but is now blocked. The Whitwell end was until recently used as a mushroom farm. Part of the railway bridge still stands at the top of Nettlecombe Lane. With the railway bringing increased transport to Whitwell, a new public house opened; this was called the Yarlborough Arms, the house is now an elderly people's home.[100]

This shows the remains of the railway bridge

A drawing of the steam train on its way to Whitwell.

During the late Victorian period Whitwell suffered from a water shortage. The red standards in the village date from this time when in 1887, when Mr Spindler of Old Park gave half the money for the standards to be put in place to provide water to the village. The rest of the money was provided by the inhabitants of Whitwell. It took nearly a year to find a suitable water supply, eventually however, it was agreed that the water should come from Mr Ward's land in Bierley. The standards are still in existence around the village and one is shown on page 66. The standpipes were in use until the late 1920s , when water was piped into houses. [101]

There were various occupations in the village during the Victorian era. Many early village shops were run as part time trades, and conducted from a cottage front room. Some cottages had large windows with big wooden shutters that could be put up as a shelter over the window and a wooden shelf that would come down to act as a counter.[102]

Agriculture was of great importance in the village. Tractors were used in the twentieth century, but before this horses would have been used to plough the fields.

This picture shows work in the fields at Ford Farm.

Haymaking was important at the end of the summer to provide food for livestock throughout the winter months.

Many of the farms would have kept livestock as well as farming crops. Livestock would produce meat, eggs and milk and wool for the family, and as a further source of income to sell to the wider community. Below is a picture of 'feeding time' at a farm in Whitwell.

The Post Office in 1859 belonged to Hannah Joliffe; the post came from Southampton via Godshill. Post Office contracts first appeared in the 1840s. Hannah Joliffe was also recorded as the schoolmistress. There was a Grocer, Francis Harvey; There are three blacksmiths; a wheelwright, James Norris; The White Horse Inn belonged to Charles Morris; There was another beer house, owned by James Woodford; a shoemaker, David Silsbury and two shopkeepers. [103]

In 1865, Hannah Joliffe is still recorded as being Postmistress and Schoolmistress. The post continued to arrive from Godshill via foot messenger. It arrived in Whitwell at 7.15 am and was collected at 5.30 pm. There is a dairy, with the dairyman recorded as William Griffin; Francis Harvey is still recorded as a shopkeeper, as is David Silsbury and a Jacob Russell. Charles Reynolds is recorded as a tailor and a shopkeeper, with Bennett Moses recorded as a carpenter. There are still three blacksmiths, and Charles Morris is now named as a farmer in addition to being the victualler of the White Horse Inn. [104]

By 1898, Windsor Colenutt had the Post office, the post now came from Ventnor by mail cart at 6.45 am, and by foot messenger at 1.00 pm. The post was dispatched at 11.00 am and 6.40 pm. The post office was now at Rose cottage. There were now wall letterboxes in Whitwell, one in the Undercliff, one near the Chapel and one at Southford Farm. Anna Harvey is now the Grocer, and there are now several dairies in Whitwell, one at Joliffe's Farm, one at Redhill with six recorded dairymen. Frederick Hibbard is the baker, at Southford, Charles Saunders is also a baker and a shopkeeper; James Copper is the station master at the newly opened Whitwell Station. Mrs George Moses is a dressmaker; James Lowe is a painter, blacksmith and contractor. The victualler for the White Horse Inn is now Ephraim Morris; John Petchey is the schoolmaster, and John Plumbley is a shoemaker and a sexton. The Directories gives evidence of a vast increase in trade and the variety of opportunities now available for the inhabitants of Whitwell. Only 2 years after the opening of the railway the village has come a long way in its trade since 1865. [105] There were other ways to earn money and a photograph of an organ grinder in Whitwell, shows that street traders worked in the smaller villages too, and not just in the towns. [106]

Poor rates had to be paid by Yeoman farmers, an example of rates that were being paid in the Victorian era are; for Godshill 1 pound 95s, for Whitwell 20s, and for St Lawrence 51s. The selling and buying of Livestock seems to have been a valuable trade, for example, 30 ewes could be brought for 30 pounds and 15 s; 3 pigs for 1 pound 8s 6d, and

50 pounds for some sheep. Livestock would also be sold and the butcher paid 3 pounds for 2 calves.

Food eaten by those on farms in and around the Whitwell area include; sugar and tea which could be brought for 3 pounds 3s. A cheese could be brought from Mrs Groves for 4s 9d, and butter for 11d per 1 lb. Different kinds of meat were also eaten; Mr Hollies supplied a leg of lamb for 4s 4d. Butcher Cooper provided 73 lbs of beef for 1 pound 13s, Veal was supplied by Mr Groves at 4 pounds 2s. Mr Cole the miller provided barley, cheese and lard for 10 pounds, 19s 1d; whereas Mr Griffin the miller supplied wheat for 19 pounds. Gingerbread could also be brought for 1 pound 9s 6d. Drink was also brought locally, a cask of brandy costing 5 pounds 6s, 4 gallons of brandy costing 6 pounds 11s 6d, and beer costing 2 pounds. Beer and ale would also be made at home. Many farms had brew and malthouses. The grocer in the village, Mr Harvey supplied tobacco at 4s for 1 lb. Many of the locals would have brought free trade brandy from the many smugglers in the area.

Medicine was brought from local people with knowledge of herbs. Chemists were also supplying medicines in the nineteenth century. Brimstone was brought at 2s 6d, whereas 'nervious' cordial was brought at 5s 5d. Services, such as pest control could also be brought. It cost about 2 ½ 5s and 11s for 2 ½ dozen moles, and for the mouse 'katcher'. Elizabeth Jacobs was paid 16s 6d for 32 days washing, and Martha Chick and her daughter paid 10s 11d for 54 days weeding. For 7 days work digging potatoes a wage of 10s 6d was paid. Mr Urry did the threshing in the fields and was paid 10s for 12 days work.

Household items such as coal, which cost 1 pound 15s 10d, and 3 bundles of laths at 10s 6d, a basket would cost about 15s and 'riting' paper about 1s; the price for clothing was approximately 12s 2d for boys shoes, 2s 6d for hose, frock and trousers cost 9s 6d. Mr Blake was also paid 1s for altering a coat. [107]

The men of Whitwell although engaged in their trades, still found the time to serve their country and during the Napoleonic Wars, men from Whitwell were prominent in the local volunteer units. The first loyal volunteer unit was raised by Captain Cole, who was the gentleman farmer of Ash and Dean Farms. This company had the title of the 'Niton Loyal Volunteers' it was made up of Whitwell and Niton volunteers. [108]

A school was run by Hannah Joliffe at the post office. In the early Victorian era, most schools were run from people's front rooms or from church or village halls; Sunday schools were sometimes run by non-conformist or dissenting groups.[109]

A school was built in Slay Lane in 1844 by the non-conformists. It suffered from money problems however, and was forced to close about 30 years later.[110] The village school being erected in 1863 with accommodation for the school master and at that time had room for 106 children. The funding from the school came from the church with the main benefactor thought to be Lady Oliver, the mother of the then Reverend. It was not until 1876 that attendance at school became compulsory, and in 1891, free education became available to all up to the age of 14. [111] The school was closed in 1944, when the children had to go to Niton School. The school today is the village hall. It was a mixed school and by the mid 20th century had places for 120 children. [112]

The school log books exist, and give an insight into life at the time for the children and what education in the early twentieth century was like in a village school.

The classes were arranged into standards; standards 4, 5, 6 and 7 were taught by Mr Petchey, standards 1, 2 and 3 were taught by Miss Willis and the infants taught by Miss Gauld in 1911. Comprehension, reading and arithmetic were taught alongside history and geography. The boys took gardening class, and drawing, the girls took sewing and knitting, with some attending a cookery class in Niton. Religious instruction was also taught, the schools strong point being the Old and New

Testaments. The image below shows the boys at one of their gardening classes. Dating from abut 1918.

The building of the school was not in great condition, and was in need of repair in the early twentieth century. The inspector's report of 1908 states that they needed more desks, improved lavatory accommodation and complains that there was only one detached basin for the whole school. [113] In 1906 the staff themselves reported that the playground was in such a state, that drill was impossible, and again in 1914, that the roof was so leaky that it interrupted the drawing lesson.[114]

A lot of the children attending the school had a long way to walk across fields and farmland to attend. This had implications if the weather was wet or very cold. There are countless accounts in the log books of attendance being low due to the bad weather. For example on Oct 13th 1903, 'Much wet weather is causing irregular attendance.' [115] The walking through the wet must have been particularly bad for the children of poor families who did not have adequate clothing and on many occasions those that had turned up in bad weather had been sent home again due to them being soaked or their feet being soaked through. It seems that this lack of attendance was causing concern, and Mr Brown, probably the attendance officer, visited the houses of those with irregular attendance. On 18th Feb. 1904, it is recorded that there was a 'snowstorm in night, Mr Brown asked teachers not to mark register on very wet days and when the attendance was small.' [116]

Attendance was a big issue at the school and in addition to the wet weather keeping class numbers down, sickness, harvesting and blackberrying played a part in low attendance. The school was closed down on at least two occasions due to illness. In August 1907, the medical officer ordered the school to close until 9th September because there were so many cases of measles in the village. On 2nd May 1915, 4 children were excluded with Whooping Cough, the next day 5 more were taken ill, and 2 more on the following day. On the 5th the school was ordered to be closed until further notice; it re-opened on the 31st May. [117]

The school had to have an incentive for keeping attendance high, and half days were awarded at monthly intervals if the attendance was good enough. On 16th May 1904, 'half day holiday because attendance in April was above 93.' On 3rd June 1904, 'half day holiday as percentage of attendance in May was 95.' [118]

It seems that if staff knew most of the children would be attending an event then half days were sometimes given or swapped about. On 31st May 1911 for example, there was a 'bazaar in village and many of the girls wish to be there.' A half day was given on this day to enable them to go and not miss school. [119] Treats were also organised for the children; on the August bank holiday in 1904, a children's tea party was held at Strathwell Park, and a summer fete. [120]

Below is a picture showing a fete in Whitwell in 1921.

Some of the children must have been attending the church in school hours, as a notice was sent to the school telling the children that they were not to attend the church during school hours. However, 13 days later the log book records that the Vicar turned up at the school at 9 am and ordered those children that attended Sunday school to go to church. There is no more mention of this matter, so one assumes that it was sorted out by some other means, although Mr Brown had taken the names of all the children that had gone with the Vicar. [121]

The school did work for the local community and played a part in the war effort helping to make socks and other items for the soldiers of the Isle of Wight who were fighting on the front line in the First World War. On the 19th Nov 1915, the school sent out 5 pairs of socks, 1 muffler and 6 pairs of cuffs for the use of Island soldiers at the front. [122] The log books show the village to be a caring community that showed consideration to others and tried to make school an enjoyable and educational experience.

# A village through time

The Whitwell of today is much changed over the centuries, but the buildings and customs still stand strong in the face of change to bring us a small part of what it was to live in Whitwell in Post-Medieval and Victorian times. The closed community that existed in the Post-Medieval period, started to open up as transport links increased. The railways brought people to and from the village and gave the villagers chances to expand their horizons. The increase in trade mirrors the new agricultural inventions and changes occurring throughout the industrial revolution.

The closing of the railway and increasing retail opportunities in the towns has led once again to a decrease in the village trades; there are now no shops, or schools in the village. The residents of Whitwell must travel out to nearby villages and towns in order to purchase their goods. Agriculture is still strong in the area, with farms, and fields continuing to surround this charming English village.

Life as a yeoman farmer and the sort of services that were offered and the food that was eaten in the early nineteenth century have been detailed to give an impression of life for the middle class farmer in the Victorian era.

Whereas, the school records give a unique insight into what it was like to be at school at the turn of the twentieth century; one can only imagine how cold and uncomfortable it would have been to sit in a classroom when you had walked a couple of miles in the rain and cold with no proper footwear. The girls had it even worse, having to walk to Niton to attend cookery classes. The community spirit is also highlighted in the making of items for the soldiers on the front line.

Whitwell was a village where everyone pulled together to help one another, a closed community to outsiders, but a warm one to its residents.

# Notes:

---

[1] Whitehead, J L *The Undercliff of the Isle of Wight past and present (London, 1911) p216*

[2] http://www.iwcp.co.uk/News/WELL_THATS_A_RAIL_CELEBRATION_2.aspx

[3] Ecclesiastical Index, Whitwell, isle of Wight Record Office

[4] Whitehead, J L *The Undercliff of the Isle of Wight past and present (London, 1911) p216*

[5] Whitehead, J L *The Undercliff of the Isle of Wight past and present (London, 1911) p215*

[6] Hinde, T, *The Domesday book: England's Heritage, then and now.* Coombe books (1996)

[7] JER/WA/33/45 and JER/WA/33/36

[8] Whitehead, J L *The Undercliff of the Isle of Wight past and present (London, 1911) p221*

9 JER/WA/33/13

[10] Deuteronomy

[11] http://dunstertithebarn.org.uk/history.htm

[12] Whitehead, J L *The Undercliff of the Isle of Wight past and present (London, 1911) p320*

[13] http://home.clara.net/brianp/money.html

[14] http://privatewww.essex.ac.uk/~alan/family/N-Money.html

[15] http://privatewww.essex.ac.uk/~alan/family/N-Money.html

[16] http://www.oldbaileyonline.org/history/london-life/coinage.html

[17] JER/WA/33/13

[18] JER/WA/18/1

[19] JER/WA/31/70

[20] JER/WA/31/23
[21] JER/WA/31/91
[22] Porter, V, *English villages*, 1992. p87
[23] JER/WA/31/24
[24] JER/WA/33/1/2
[25] JER/BAR/3/11/1
[26] JER/WA/18/6a & b
[27] JER/WA/32/74
[28] BD 220
[29] JER/WA/18/12a & b
[30] JER/WA/31/18
[31] JER/WA/18/5
[32] JER/WA/31/28
[33] JER/WA/33/11
[34] JER/WA/33/25
[35] JER/WA/83/1/2
[36] JER/WA/31/30
[37] JER/WA/31/39
[38] JER/BAR/3/11/1
[39] JER/WA/33/11
[40] JER/WA/33/25
[41] JER/WA/83/1/2
[42] JER/WA/33/11
[43] JER/WA/33/25
[44] JER/WA/31/67
[45] JER/WA/18/1
[46] JER/WA/18/4
[47] JER/WA/31/72
[48] The recollections of Old John Green, I.W. Mercury 1890
[49] JER/WA/18/4
[50] JER/WA/83/1/2
[51] JER/WA/33/11
[52] Ventnor and District Local history Society Inns and Ale Bonchurch to Chale.' 1985
[53] JER/WA/31/36

[54] JER/WA/33/25
[55] Kellys Directory 1921-22 and 1923
[56]Porter, V, *English villages*, 1992. p83
[57] BD 220
[58] BD221
[59] Whitehead, J L *The Undercliff of the Isle of Wight past and present (London, 1911) p342*
[60] Porter, V, *English villages*, 1992. p19
[61] Porter, V, *English villages*, 1992. p117
[62] JER/WA/33/1/2
[63] JER/WA/33/11
[64] JER/WA/33/25
[65] Kellys Directory 1898
[66] Whitehead, J L *The Undercliff of the Isle of Wight past and present (London, 1911)p253*
[67] 'Parishes: Whitwell', A History of the County of Hampshire: Volume 5 (1912), pp. 202-04. URL: http://www.british-history.ac.uk/report.asp?compid=42074. Date accessed: 16 August 2007.
[68] Whitehead, J L *The Undercliff of the Isle of Wight past and present (London, 1911)p254*
[69] Moncrieft A R Hope, Isle of Wight, (1908)
[70] Hooper, P, *Our Island, in war and commonwealth. (*Chale, 1998) p98
[71] ibid
[72] 'Parishes: Whitwell', A History of the County of Hampshire: Volume 5 (1912), pp. 202-04. URL: http://www.british-history.ac.uk/report.asp?compid=42074. Date accessed: 16 August 2007.
[73]
http://www.iwcp.co.uk/News/WELL_DRESSING_MAKES_A_COMEBACK.aspx
[74] Alexander, M, *Folklore, Myths and customs of Britain.* 2002

[75] http://www.iwcp.co.uk/News/WELL_THATS_A_RAIL_CELEBRATION_2.aspx
[76] 21M65/F2/3/25
[77] 21M65/F2/3/363
[78] 21M65/F2/4/117
[79] 21M65/F2/4/145
[80] 21M65/F2/5/111
[81] Kelly's Directory 1898
[82] Porter, V, *English villages*, 1992. p91
[83] The recollections of Old John Green, I.W. Mercury 1890
[84] http://www.apotropaios.co.uk/
[85] http://www.orkneyjar.com/tradition/yule/yule2.htm
[86] Sieveking, P, 'Death is kept at bay by the skulls of a cow', *Sunday Telegraph*, September 12 th 1999.
[87] Index of shoes at Northampton museum
[88] Dixon-Smith D, *Concealed shoes,* Archaeological Leather Group Newsletter No.6 Spring 1990
[89] JER/WA/33/13
[90] The recollections of Old John Green, I.W. Mercury 1890
[91] Whitehead, J L *The Undercliff of the Isle of Wight past and present (London, 1911)p258*
[92] Brannon, *Pleasure visitor's companion to the Isle of Wight* (1876)
[93] Directory of Hampshire and the Isle of Wight, 1859
[94] Harrod & Co.'s Directory of Hampshire & Isle of Wight, 1865
[95] Kellys Directory 1898
[96] Porter, V, *English villages*, 1992. p115
[97] http://www.railscot.co.uk/Ventnor_Branch/frame.htm
98 Maycock,RJ, Silsbury, R, *The IOW Central Railway* (Oakwood press, 2001)
[99] Harding, P, *The Ventnor West Branch Line*, Surrey, 1990

[100] Ventnor and District Local history Society Inns and Ale Bonchurch to Chale.' 1985
[101] Jarratt, P E, *Whitwell, An island village.p6*
[102] Porter, V, *English villages*, 1992. p119
[103] Directory of Hampshire and the Isle of Wight, 1859
[104] Harrod & Co.'s Directory of Hampshire & Isle of Wight, 1865
[105] Kellys Directory 1898
[106] Scammell, *H, Rural Wight in Bygone days*, 1982
[107] Private collection
[108] The recollections of Old John Green, I.W. Mercury 1890
[109] Porter, V, *English villages*, 1992. p93
[110] Jarratt, P E, *Whitwell, An island village, p9*
[111] Porter, V, *English villages*, 1992. p97
[112] Kellys Directory 1898
[113] Whitwell school log book iwcc/ed/g/8/1
[114] ibid
[57]Ibid.
[116] Ibid.
[117] Ibid.
[118] Ibid.
[119] Ibid.
[120] Ibid.
[121] Ibid.
[122] Ibid

# Bibliography

## Primary sources:

JER/WA/33/36: Survey of Worsley Estate 1772-1803

JER/WA/33/45: Worsley Estate Map 1773

JER/WA/33/13: Worsley stewards account books 1714

JER/WA/18/1: Whitwell lease 1560

JER/WA/32/74: copy of Whitwell manor court roll 1674

BD 220: index card in Whitwell section of Record office

JER/WA/18/12a & b : Whitwell lease 1638

JER/WA/31/18 : Whitwell lease 1638

JER/WA/31/70: lease for Guys cottage and shoemakers shop 1802

JER/WA/31/91: Whitwell lease 1615

JER/WA/31/23 : lease on Kemming 1675

JER/WA/31/24 : lease for church house 1680

JER/WA/33/1/2: Worsley stewards account books 1677

JER/WA/18/6a & b: Whitwell lease 1780

JER/WA/18/5: Whitwell lease 1688

JER/WA/31/28: lease on Pells smith shop 1699

JER/WA/33/11: Worsley stewards account books 1712

JER/WA/33/25: Worsley stewards account books 1778

JER/WA/83/1/2: Worsley stewards account books 1676

JER/WA/31/30 : lease on Southford 1703

JER/WA/31/39: lease on Southford mill 1729

JER/BAR/3/11/1: leases 1773

JER/WA/31/67 : lease on Chiddles 1780

JER/WA/18/4: partition of manor of Whitwell 1596

JER/WA/31/72 : lease on White Horse 1802

JER/WA/31/36 : lease on church house 1723

Whitwell school log book iwcc/ed/g/8/1 : IOW county education committee log book 1903-1924

The recollections of Old John Green, I.W. Mercury 1890

Brannon, *Pleasure visitor's companion to the Isle of Wight* (1876)

Directory of Hampshire and the Isle of Wight, 1859

Harrod & Co.'s Directory of Hampshire & Isle of Wight, 1865

Hill and co Historical and commercial directory of the IOW, 1871

Kellys Directory 1898

Kellys Directory 1921-22 and 1923

Deuteronomy, The Holy Bible

Private collection

## Secondary sources:

Alexander, M, *Folklore, Myths and customs of Britain.* 2002

Dixon-Smith D, *Concealed shoes,* Archaeological Leather Group Newsletter No.6 Spring 1990

Harding, P, *The Ventnor West Branch Line*, Surrey, 1990

Hinde, T, *The Domesday book: England's Heritage, then and now.* Coombe books (1996)

Hooper, P, *Our Island, in war and commonwealth. (*Chale, 1998)

Jarratt, P E, *Whitwell, An island village (Chale)*

Maycock,RJ, Silsbury, R, *The IOW Central Railway* (Oakwood press, 2001)

Moncrieft A R Hope, *Isle of Wight*, 1908

Porter, V, *English villages*, 1992.

Scammell, *H, Rural Wight in Bygone days*, 1982

Ventnor and District Local history Society '*Inns and Ale Bonchurch to Chale.*' 1985

## Websites:

http://www.railscot.co.uk/Ventnor_Branch/frame.htm

'Parishes: Whitwell', A History of the County of Hampshire: Volume 5 (1912), pp. 202-04. URL: http://www.british-history.ac.uk/report.asp?compid=42074. Date accessed: 16 August 2007.

http://www.oldbaileyonline.org/history/london-life/coinage.html

http://privatewww.essex.ac.uk/~alan/family/N-Money.html

http://home.clara.net/brianp/money.html

http://dunstertithebarn.org.uk/history.htm

http://www.iwcp.co.uk/News/WELL_DRESSING_MAKES_A_COMEBACK.aspx

http://www.iwcp.co.uk/News/WELL_THATS_A_RAIL_CELEBRATION_2.aspx

http://www.apotropaios.co.uk/

http://www.orkneyjar.com/tradition/yule/yule2.htm

# The author

**This is Joanne Thornton's second book. Her first book being a local history study on Women's crime in Hertfordshire, titled 'Criminal Women in early 17th century Hertfordshire.' It was published by Trafford in 2004.**
**Joanne has a BA (Hons) degree in History from the University of Hertfordshire and is currently studying toward an MA Archaeology and Heritage with the University of Leicester.**

www.ingramcontent.com/pod-product-compliance
Ingram Content Group UK Ltd.
Pitfield, Milton Keynes, MK11 3LW, UK
UKHW040558210726
13854UKWH00008B/1474

9 781409 258520